I BELIEVE

I Can Learn Something New, Just Like Cody, the Best Dog Swimmer

Coloring and Activity Book 5

SUZANNE MONDOUX
Illustrated by Gaëtanne Mondoux

BALBOA PRESS
A DIVISION OF HAY HOUSE

Balboa Press books may be ordered through booksellers or by contacting:

Balboa Press
A Division of Hay House
1663 Liberty Drive
Bloomington, IN 47403
www.balboapress.com
1 (877) 407-4847

Because of the dynamic nature of the Internet, any web addresses or links contained in this book may have changed since publication and may no longer be valid. The views expressed in this work are solely those of the author and do not necessarily reflect the views of the publisher, and the publisher hereby disclaims any responsibility for them.

The author of this book does not dispense medical advice or prescribe the use of any technique as a form of treatment for physical, emotional, or medical problems without the advice of a physician, either directly or indirectly. The intent of the author is only to offer information of a general nature to help you in your quest for emotional and spiritual well-being. In the event you use any of the information in this book for yourself, which is your constitutional right, the author and the publisher assume no responsibility for your actions.

Any people depicted in stock imagery provided by Getty Images are models, and such images are being used for illustrative purposes only.
Certain stock imagery © Getty Images.

Print information available on the last page.

ISBN: 978-1-9822-2266-6 (sc)
ISBN: 978-1-9822-2279-6 (e)

Balboa Press rev. date: 02/22/2019

This book belongs to

_____

I am _____ years old

Carlo and Teddy walked for days and days on the trail looking for their next adventure. They walked through the forest, across open fields and up and down hills and into valleys. They galloped in the streams and played in the water.

One day they came upon sand dunes that stretched forever one way and forever the other way. They ran to the highest dune and looked out onto the sea. The wind was blowing loudly and the waves were crashing against the shore as loud as thunder.

It was late in the afternoon and they had not stopped to eat their lunch yet. They found a perfect spot on the beach where they were a little protected from the wind. In a tiny nook between two dunes was a nice flat spot in the sparse grass in the sand to have a picnic.

There they ate quietly, enjoying the majestic beauty of the sea that went on and on forever everywhere they looked. The sun was shining bright and orange in the sky over the horizon.

Suddenly, their peaceful lunch was interrupted with a loud bark coming from far away on the other end of the beach. They looked as far as they could to where the dunes curved back up the tiny hill. A tiny cloud of sand rose above a tiny grey dog running towards them.

The tiny grey dog ran very fast. He wagged his tail and barked and barked and barked with joy. Then he turned towards the sea and leaped right into the waves. He swam in and out of the waves and let the waves carry him back onto the beach. Then he would run back into the water and do it all over again. He did this over and over again until he saw Carlo and Teddy standing on the beach next to where the waves had rolled him to shore.

All wet and sandy the tiny grey dog shook his fur vigorously to free the sand from his body. Water and sand sprayed Carlo and Teddy in the face. They neighed and shook their heads left to right.

"Hello, welcome to my beach," said the little grey dog. "My name is Cody. What is your name? Would you like to come for a swim? Do you know how to swim? If you do not know how to swim I can teach you?"

"Hello, please one question at a time," said Teddy. Carlo and Teddy could see Cody was very excited to have met them. He was full of life and joy and was so happy that he could swim and play in the sea.

"Hello," said Cody.

"Hello, my name is Carlo and this is my friend Teddy." Cody raised his right paw and touched their right hooves. "Welcome, horses. It is a pleasure to have you here. Shall we go swimming?" Cody wagged his tail and turned to face the sea. "Lets go!"

"Excuse me. Excuse me Cody," said Teddy.

"Yes, what is it?"

"I do not know how to swim. I have never been near the sea before and I have never been in the sea." Teddy lowered his head, embarrassed that he did not know how to swim.

Carlo did not know this about his friend. He was also a stranger to the sea and to swimming in the sea. "I do not know how to swim either," said Carlo.

Cody looked up at them. He stepped a little closer and stood in front of them. "There is no need to be embarrassed about not knowing how to swim. I will show you. There are many horses, animals and people who do not know how to swim or have never seen the sea or been in the sea. I believe there is no time like the present to learn to do something new if it is something you want to learn and do. Are you interested in learning how to swim in the sea?"

Teddy looked down at Cody and back up at the sea. "Yes, I want to learn how to swim in the sea." He looked at Carlo waiting for his answer.

Carlo stared out at the sea. The waves were crashing up against his feet. The water sprayed and splashed his face. He licked the salt water from his lips. "I am afraid of what I can't see beneath the water. How do I know I will not sink right to the bottom?"

Cody walked into the waves as they rolled onto the shore. "I will teach you everything there is to know about water safety and swimming. You should always learn water safety and how to swim before going in the sea."

Cody stepped back onto the beach. He pointed to flags bobbing in and out of the water.

"Rule #1. Always swim between the flags marking the zone you can swim. Swim where you know you can see a lifeguard and a lifeguard can see you." He pointed to the lifeguard in the distance sitting in her chair scanning the beach and the sea through her binoculars.

"Rule #2. Never swim alone in case you get into difficulty." Cody pointed to his leg. "I had a cramp in my leg once when I was swimming. I was happy my swimming buddy was next to me. She helped me out of the water."

"Rule # 3. If you think the sea is too rough, do not go in. It is important to know how good of a swimmer you are, and it is being sensible to know when you could put yourself and others in danger." He walked into the water. "Today the sea is not too rough. It is a good day for swimming."

"Rule # 4. If you are doing a longer swim, then swim along the shoreline, not out to the sea and back. If you get tired or into difficulty, you have a chance of getting back to the shore, or the lifeguard can see you and help you if you need." Cody ran along the shoreline wagging his tail in the water.

"Rule #5. Do not swim after dark, as no one can see you if you need help. We have a few more hours before it gets dark." He pointed to the sun setting in the west behind the sand dunes.

"Rule # 6. If you hear a siren, or the lifeguard tells you to get out of the water, GET OUT AT ONCE. They know what they are doing and they give you their time to keep you safe."

Carlo and Teddy repeated the six (6) rules. They looked at each other and considered everything Cody had told them.

"Ok, we are ready to learn how to swim today," said Teddy.

For the rest of the day Carlo and Teddy followed every instruction and did everything Cody taught them. Before they knew it they were swimming on their own along the shoreline. With their head above water they propelled themselves forward by moving their legs as if trotting. They laughed and played in the water until it was time to get out of the water just before sun set.

Back on the beach Carlo and Teddy shook the water from their bodies. They kicked their back feet up in the air with joy. They played in the sand and ran after each other.

Cody ran behind them and played with them a little while longer.

"Cody, thank you for showing us how to swim. I had a really fun day!" said Teddy.

"Me too. I had a really fun day," said Carlo. Thank you for showing me how to swim. I didn't know how much fun you can have swimming. I only wish I had learned how to swim a long time ago. But now I know and I am very proud of myself."

Cody stood very proud that he made someone else happy. He was happy that he could help somebody else and teach them something new.

"Follow me," shouted Cody. "Come this way."

Carlo and Teddy trotted behind Cody. They jumped over a sand dune next to a big doghouse made of wood and grass. "This is my home. You can spend the night over there on the beach. But first we can have some dinner and watch stars light up the night sky."

Cody prepared their dinner. They talked about their adventures, people and animals they met along the way.

"There are many things I would like to learn to do," said Carlo.

"Me too, I would love to learn many things I have only read about," said Teddy.

"Then you need to find out who can teach you, and decide when you want to learn all these new things you want to learn to do," said Cody.

Cody pulled out a piece of paper and pencil from his doghouse and placed it on a stone. "Make a list of everything that interests you. Write down what you want to learn to do."

"Thank you Cody, that is a really good idea," said Teddy.

"Before we go to bed tonight we will think about what we each want to write in our list," said Carlo.

"Wonderful! Let your imagination take you wherever it want's to take you. There are no limits to what you can learn and desire," said Cody. Cody shook the sand from his feet and wished them good night. He walked into his doghouse and blew out the candle.

Carlo and Teddy stared up at the stars. They talked about everything they wanted to learn.

By the time they had finished their list there wasn't anywhere else to write on the piece of paper. They read it out loud one last time before they yawned and yawned and fell asleep beneath the starry sky, with their minds and hearts filled with all sorts of new dreams.

List

volunteer at an animal shelter

discover what's in a pond

run through a sprinkler

go tandem skydiving

go Zorbing

sing Karaoke

canoe down a river

light a fire without matches

Cody invites you to write a list of everything that is of interest to you, and that you would like to learn.

For the next 30 days

Write one thing you want to learn. Write what you need to do to learn what interest you, and write what you will do to make certain you learn it.

On another page find the name of an animal that lives in the sea. Write one thing you learned about this animal.

_____

_____

_____

_____

_____

_____

_____

_____

_____

_____

_____

_____

Draw a picture of the animal.

Lets begin.

Most importantly - Have fun!

Remember to smile.

Remember to laugh.

Remember to be curious and ask questions.

Remember to Believe in yourself.

Say out loud 10 times.

I Believe in myself.
I Believe in myself.
I Believe in myself.
I Believe in myself.
I Believe in myself.
I Believe in myself.
I Believe in myself.
I Believe in myself.
I Believe in myself.
I Believe in myself.

Day 1

Day 2

Day 3

_____

_____

_____

_____

_____

_____

_____

_____

_____

_____

_____

_____

_____

Day 4

_____

_____

_____

_____

_____

_____

_____

_____

_____

_____

_____

_____

Day 5

Day 6

_____

_____

_____

_____

_____

_____

_____

_____

_____

_____

_____

_____

_____

Day 7

_____

_____

_____

_____

_____

_____

_____

_____

_____

_____

_____

Day 8

_____

_____

_____

_____

_____

_____

_____

_____

_____

_____

_____

_____

Day 9

Day 10

Day 11

_____

_____

_____

_____

_____

_____

_____

_____

_____

_____

_____

_____

Day 12

_____

_____

_____

_____

_____

_____

_____

_____

_____

_____

_____

_____

Day 13

_____

_____

_____

_____

_____

_____

_____

_____

_____

_____

_____

_____

_____

Day 14

_____

_____

_____

_____

_____

_____

_____

_____

_____

_____

_____

_____

Day 15

_____

_____

_____

_____

_____

_____

_____

_____

_____

_____

_____

_____

Day 16

_____

_____

_____

_____

_____

_____

_____

_____

_____

_____

_____

_____

_____

Day 17

_____

_____

_____

_____

_____

_____

_____

_____

_____

_____

_____

_____

Day 18

Day 19

_____

_____

_____

_____

_____

_____

_____

_____

_____

_____

_____

_____

Day 20

_____

_____

_____

_____

_____

_____

_____

_____

_____

_____

_____

_____

Day 21

_____

_____

_____

_____

_____

_____

_____

_____

_____

_____

_____

_____

Day 22

_____

_____

_____

_____

_____

_____

_____

_____

_____

_____

_____

_____

Day 23

_____

_____

_____

_____

_____

_____

_____

_____

_____

_____

_____

Day 24

Day 25

_____

_____

_____

_____

_____

_____

_____

_____

_____

_____

_____

Day 26

Day 27

_____

_____

_____

_____

_____

_____

_____

_____

_____

_____

_____

_____

_____

Day 28

Day 29

Day 30

WOW! YOU ARE AMAZING!!!!!!!!!!!!!!

YOU DID ALL THE FUN STUFF!

YOU PARTICIPATED IN 30 DAYS OF FUN!

KEEP GOING!

EXPLORE YOUR IMAGINATION!

BELIEVE IN YOURSELF ALWAYS!

SHARE WHAT YOU WANT TO LEARN, HOW YOU'RE GOING TO LEARN IT, WHAT YOU WILL DO TO MAKE CERTAIN THAT YOU LEARN IT, AND THE EXPLORATION OF YOUR IMAGINATION WITH A FRIEND!

THANK YOU FOR BEING GOOD AND KIND TO EVERY ANIMAL.

On behalf of all the ANIMALS – thank you for making this a better world for ALL OF US!